The Butterfly and I

Vannaly Li

To my family and friends with love

One joyful June afternoon, a beautiful butterfly
fluttered by.
I stopped playing as I could hardly believe my eyes!

When it landed on the front wall of my townhome,
I wanted to chase it for fun but decided to leave
it alone.

I watched its wings spread out, sunbathing,
As I quietly approached it to enjoy a
close-up viewing.

I marveled at the unique pattern of this
colorful insect.
I then made a promise to treat it with respect.

The butterfly seemed so calm and carefree.
Its mere presence filled my heart with glee.

The next day I rushed home after gym class
was done.
The sky was still lit by the bright summer sun.

Curious to see if the butterfly had returned to the
same place,
I quickly ran to check the front yard just in case.

I cried to my mother in disbelief,
As I spotted the butterfly on a green leaf!

My mother was so surprised; she beamed
in delight,
When she saw the butterfly bask in the sunlight.

Oh, I was so happy to see the butterfly this
second time.
I thought for a while, deciding to name it Ellie Mine.

Curiosity made me want to better know my new friend.
So time with her, I would spend.

HOME IS WHEREVER I'M WITH YOU

I told my big brother about the butterfly that visited twice.
He didn't believe me and kept eating broccoli and rice.

During research, we learned that Ellie Mine is a red admiral butterfly.
Butterflies like her can be found in warm places under a blue sky.

This charming butterfly even tastes with her feet!
Do you know what red admiral butterflies eat?

They use their tongues to sip from ripe fruits and flower nectar.
Would you believe that Ellie Mine was once a caterpillar?

The sight of my butterfly friend surprised my big brother!
We made a rule to not touch, scare, or be butterfly catchers!

Ellie would fly around and over our heads. Sometimes she would land as if our hair was her bed!

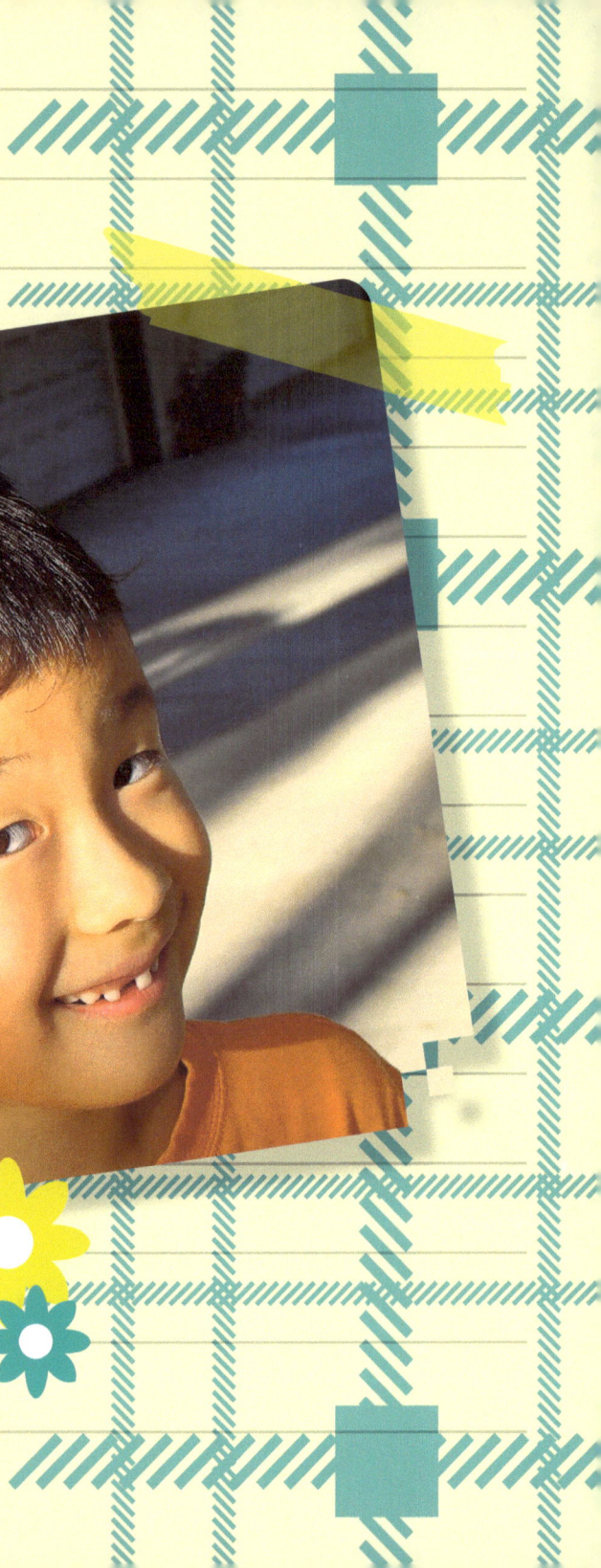

She was super friendly, landing on us with no fear.
Every time she did that, we grinned from ear to ear.

When we placed our hands near her, she would linger.
She sometimes rested one leg on our finger.

Was this her way of tasting or giving us a handshake?
She was both curious and friendly, make no mistake.

Once my brother and I rolled our pink and blue balls down the driveway hill,
Ellie Mine chased them, filling our hearts with laughter and thrill!

Ellie protected her area and battled other butterflies;
Yet, she was not disturbed by ants when they passed by.

Ellie Mine spent about two hours at our home.
We wondered where else did she roam?

She came to our front yard around 5 p.m.
each day.
Though she did not have a watch, she's quite
punctual, I'd say.

As the summer days faded into
autumn weather,
She started coming at around 4 p.m.
in September.

One early October day, Ellie Mine did not follow
her regular schedule.
Even a light drizzle in Los Angeles was
quite unusual.

When Mom and I came home from the
shopping mall,
I spotted Ellie Mine perching on the
retaining wall.

"Oh no," I thought, "her wings will get wet."
I quickly grabbed an umbrella to protect my pet.

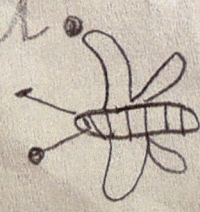

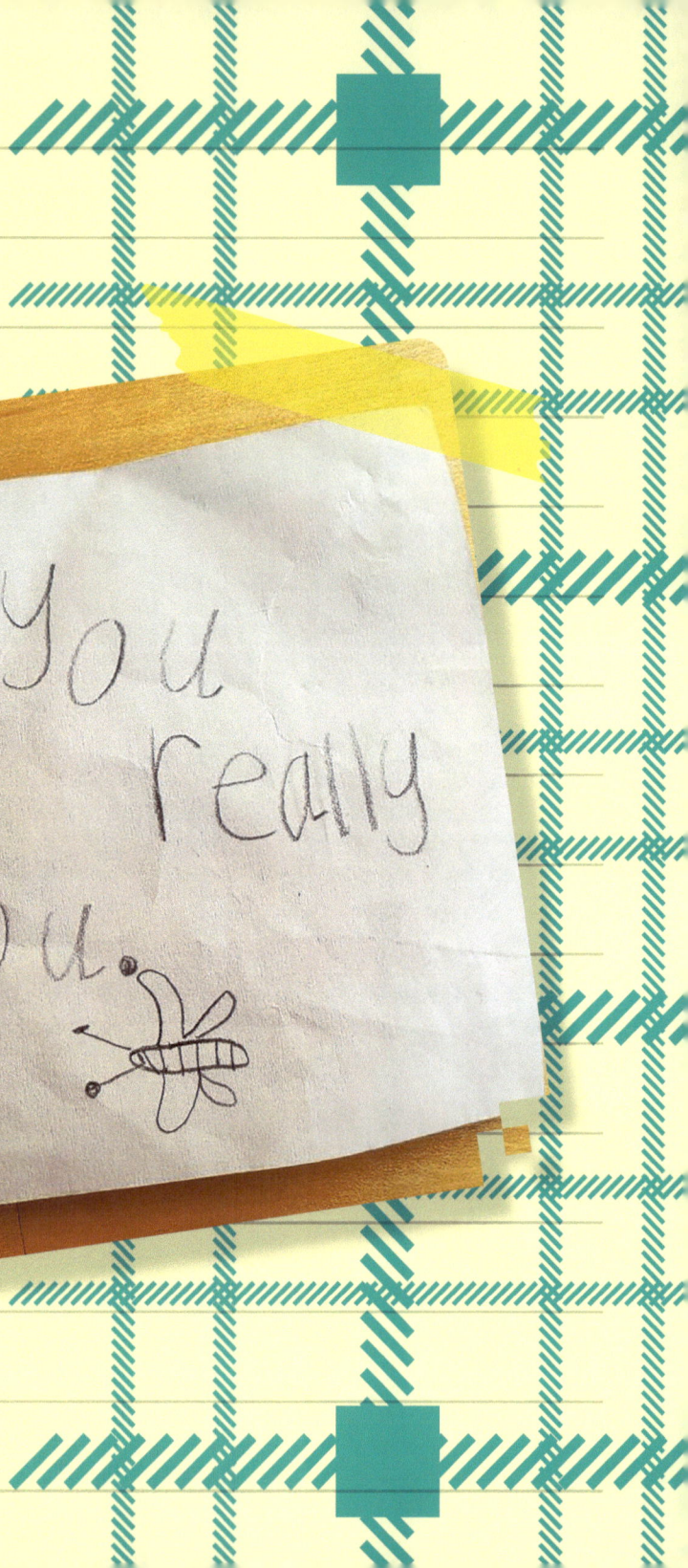

I stood with my umbrella over her that day,
Remaining there until she fluttered away.

I went outside the next day, and Ellie Mine was not there.
The autumn breeze brought a coldness into the air.

Even though we knew that she would leave from the start,
It didn't prepare us for the emptiness we felt in our hearts.

Mom explained as the winter months unfold,
Ellie must migrate or hibernate to protect herself from
the cold.

It was not easy when Ellie Mine said goodbye.
My brother and I missed our sweet butterfly.

We realized that our time with Ellie Mine was a treasure.
Our gratitude for her friendship was beyond measure.

Eight months passed by when we realized that
Ellie had left a special gift.
She left us a baby just like her to give us a lift!

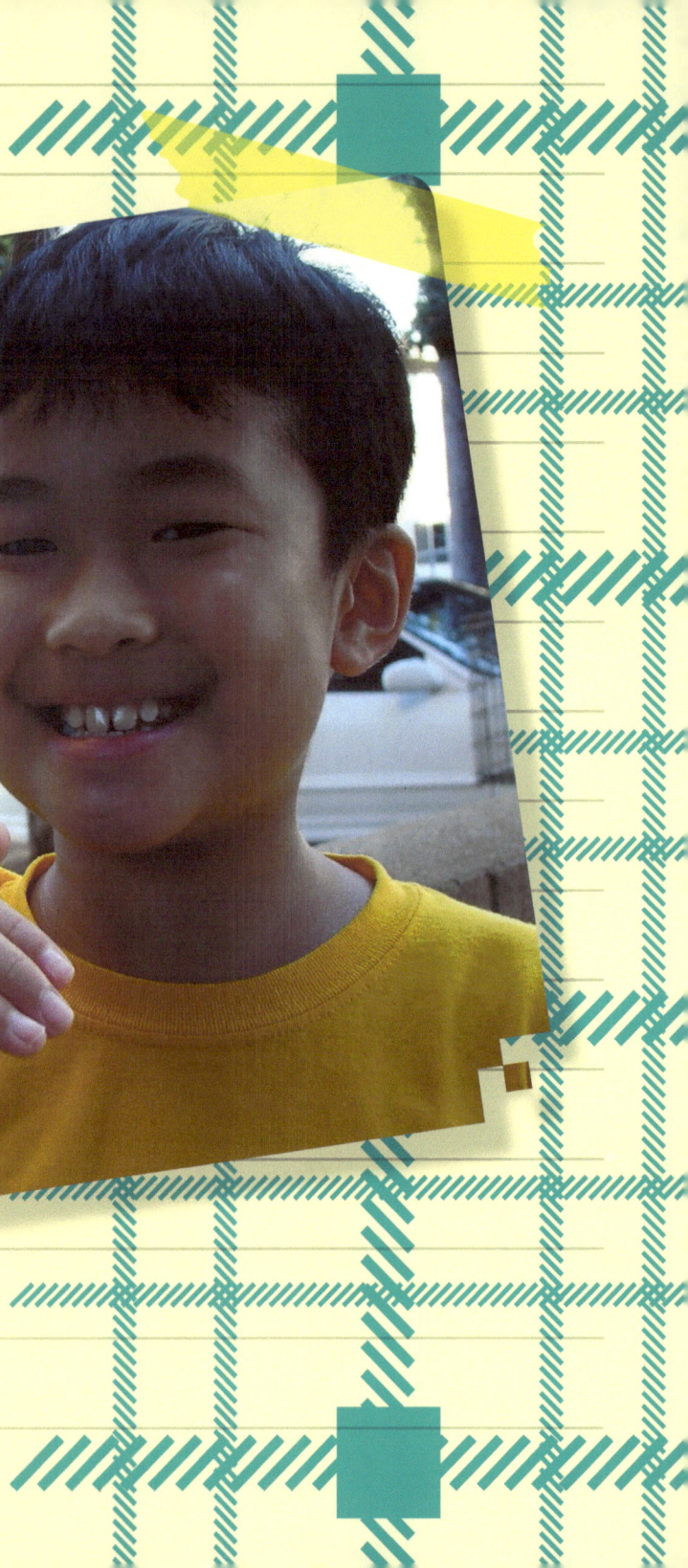

Acknowledgments

I would like to thank my children, Chloe and Tyler, who inspired me to write this book. I am also grateful to Ms. Lisa Carpenter, Mr. Curtis Duong, and Jamie C. McHugh for their support and editing contributions.